Jane
Goodall

Read These Other
Ferguson Career Biographies

Maya Angelou
Author and
Documentary Filmmaker
by Lucia Raatma

Leonard Bernstein
Composer and Conductor
by Jean F. Blashfield

Shirley Temple Black
Actor and Diplomat
by Jean F. Blashfield

George Bush
Business Executive
and U.S. President
by Robert Green

Bill Gates
Computer Programmer
and Entrepreneur
by Lucia Raatma

John Glenn
Astronaut and U.S. Senator
by Robert Green

Martin Luther King Jr.
Minister and
Civil Rights Activist
by Brendan January

Charles Lindbergh
Pilot
by Lucia Raatma

Sandra Day O'Connor
Lawyer and
Supreme Court Justice
by Jean Kinney Williams

Wilma Rudolph
Athlete and Educator
by Alice K. Flanagan

Jane Goodall

Animal Behaviorist and Writer

BRENDAN JANUARY

Ferguson Publishing Company
Chicago, Illinois

JB
Goodall

Photographs ©: Lee/Archive Photos, cover; Fotos International/Archive Photos, 8; Alfred Hind Robinson/Archive Photos, 13; Fox Photos/Archive Photos, 16; Hulton-Deutsch Collection/Corbis, 22; AP/Wide World Photos, 24; Kennan Ward/Corbis, 30; Ron Levy/Liaison Agency, 32; Express Newspapers/Archive Photos, 34; Jane Goodall/National Geographic Society Image Collection, 40; Kenneth Love/National Geographic Society Image Collection, 41; Michael Nichols/National Geographic Society Image Collection, 44; Hugo van Lawick/National Geographic Society Image Collection, 48; Kenneth Love/National Geographic Society Image Collection, 53; Hugo van Lawick/National Geographic Society Image Collection, 56; Fotos International/Archive Photos, 60; Morris-Goodall/National Geographic Society Image Collection, 64; Archive Photos, 66; Bettmann/Corbis, 68; Hugo van Lawick/National Geographic Society Image Collection, 73; Archive Photos, 78; Penelope Breese/Liaison Agency, 87, 89; Charles Bennett/AP/Wide World Photos, 90; Jean-Marc Bouju/AP/Wide World Photos, 97.

An Editorial Directions Book
Library of Congress Cataloging-in-Publication Data
January, Brendan, 1972–
    Jane Goodall / by Brendan January
    p. cm.— (A Ferguson career biography)
    Includes bibliographical references (p.).
    ISBN 0-89434-370-X
    1. Goodall, Jane, 1934– —Juvenile literature.
2.Primatologists—England—Biography—Juvenile literature. 3. Chimpanzees—Tanzania—Gombe Stream National Park—Juvenile literature. [1. Goodall, Jane, 1934– 2. Zoologists. 3. Women—Biography. 4. Chimpanzees.] I. Title. II. Ferguson career biographies.
QL31.G58 J36 2001
590'.92—dc21
[B]   00-049041

Copyright © 2001 by Ferguson Publishing Company
Published and distributed by
Ferguson Publishing Company
200 West Jackson Boulevard, Suite 700
Chicago, Illinois 60606
www.fergpubco.com

30652001022062

CONTENTS

Protector of nature. Even as a young woman, Jane Goodall loved the natural world and all the animals in it.

IN LOVE WITH NATURE

Jane Goodall, who would spend much of her life beneath the leafy canopy of an African forest, was born in a hospital in London, England, on April 3, 1934. Jane's father, Mortimer Herbert Morris-Goodall, was an engineer. Her mother, Margaret Myfanwe Joseph, wrote novels under the name Vanne Goodall.

No one can explain how or why, but from the first days of her childhood, Jane was passionate about animals of all kinds. When Jane was only a year old, her father bought her a stuffed animal—a chimpanzee named

Jubilee. Friends of the family predicted that the hairy toy, almost bigger than Jane, would terrify her. But Jane was delighted with Jubilee, and he became her constant companion.

Jane wasn't attracted to only cute, cuddly animals; she found all life interesting. Every animal she could find near her London home drew her gaze—birds, cats, dogs, and insects. When she was eighteen months old, Jane scooped up a bunch of earthworms from the garden and carried them to bed with her. Jane's mother, Vanne, found them wriggling beneath Jane's pillow.

"Jane, if you keep them here they'll die," she said. "They need the earth." Jane hurried to return the worms to the garden.

At the tender age of four, Jane provided the first glimpse of her scientific genius. In 1938, she visited her grandmother's farm. Jane was given the job of collecting freshly laid eggs from hens each day. As she went about her task, the young girl was puzzled. The hen's body had no opening large enough to release an egg. Where did the egg come from? She asked adults, but no one gave her a satisfying answer. So the four-year-old decided to solve the mystery on her own.

Intending to watch a hen lay an egg, she followed one into the hen house. But the terrified bird fled from the girl. The setback didn't discourage Jane. She realized that she would have to hide first and wait for a hen to lay an egg. With that plan in mind, Jane slithered into the corner of another henhouse, covered herself with a layer of straw, and waited. And waited. Four hours later, a hen settled into a nest right in front of her. Holding her breath, Jane watched an egg slide out of the feathers between the hen's legs and land in the straw.

Delighted, Jane slid out of the henhouse and ran to tell her mother what she had seen. While Jane had been in hiding, the entire household had been searching for her. Even the police had been called. But Vanne did not scold Jane when she saw her running toward her. Vanne recognized that the child had seen something special, and she did not want to crush Jane's joy with a harsh reprimand.

"[Vanne] did not scold me," wrote Jane in her memoir, *Reason for Hope.* "She noticed my shining eyes and sat down to listen to the story of how a hen lays an egg." Today, Jane credits her mother for nurturing her love of nature and giving her the discipline to study it.

War and Life at the Birches

When Jane was five, the family moved to France. Jane's father hoped that Jane and her one-year-old sister, Judy, would grow up to speak fluent French. But Europe in the late 1930s was falling beneath the shadow of war. Adolf Hitler and the Nazis had taken control of Germany and were occupying countries in Eastern Europe. The Goodall family soon returned to England.

Because they had sold their house before moving to France, the Goodalls settled with Mortimer Goodall's family. They lived in an ancient stone country estate without electricity or central heating. Jane loved it. Geese roamed freely on the lawn. Jane watched farmers do their chores and she explored the crumbling ruins of a historic sixteenth-century castle.

When war finally broke out in 1939, Jane's father joined the British Army, and Jane, her sister, and her mother then moved in with Vanne's mother at the Birches, a handsome brick house on the coast of southern England near the resort town of Bournemouth. The beautiful home was just a few minutes from dramatic beaches and cliffs on the English Channel. The backyard was surrounded by

A nearby park. Jane Goodall spent part of her childhood in the small town of Bournemouth.

thick hedges, and in the garden stood a beech tree where Jane spent hours resting and doing homework in its branches.

While Jane enjoyed the Birches, the war intensified, engulfing Europe and the United States. The house filled up—with Jane's two aunts, an uncle, and two single women who were left homeless by the war.

German airplanes roared over England, dropping bombs on cities as well as military installations. Though Jane's town was never a target, stray German bombs landed nearby, their deafening explosions sometimes cracking the windows at the Birches. The wailing of an air-raid siren sent the occupants of the house hurrying to a cramped, steel shelter until the all-clear siren sounded.

In the beauty of the Birches, Jane found consolation from the war. She watched with joy the birds assembling twigs and grass into nests, spiders carrying egg sacs, and squirrels chasing one another from tree to tree. Jane and her sister also kept snails in a box with a glass top and no bottom. When the snails had eaten all the dandelion leaves in one spot, the girls would move the box to a fresh patch of grass. The girls also painted numbers on the snail shells. Jane and Judy would then watch them "race" down a 6-foot (2-meter) track.

Jane, Judy, and two friends who summered at the Birches formed a group called the Alligator Society. Sometimes, Jane would lead the girls on hikes to the nearby cliffs, where she would scrawl descriptions of the wildlife and identify animals in books after returning home. Other times, the club met in a little clearing behind some dense bushes. There, they boiled water in a tin set over a fire and enjoyed mugs of cocoa and scraps of bread and biscuits saved from meals.

Jane also loved reading. One volume especially influenced the seven-year-old—*The Story of Dr. Dolittle*, by Hugh Lofting. The book tells about a doctor who can speak with and understand animals. Jane read it three times in a row—the last time by flashlight under a blanket after her mother had sent her to bed. She found the story irresistible. Jane wanted to be like Dr. Dolittle and have his powers of communication with animals.

Jane was also thrilled by the Tarzan books by Edgar Rice Burroughs, about a human hero raised by apes in Africa. Later, Jane wrote that her readings about Dr. Dolittle and Tarzan gave her a powerful dream—to visit Africa.

In the meantime, the war continued. Jane later wrote that she was too young to understand what was happening around her, but by the time she was seven, she was used to the constant reports of battles, victories, and defeats. And her memory is seared by images of the war: the radio announcement that the war had begun, an American soldier who became a friend and later died in combat, and the horror of the Nazi death camps where millions of Jews were killed.

Shortly after the war ended in 1945, Jane's father

An English street after a German bombing. Jane Goodall grew up during the violence of World War II.

and mother divorced. Jane continued to live at the Birches with her mother and her family.

Jane entered school, where she became one of the top students. But while she enjoyed studying some subjects, she felt confined and stifled in the classroom. She longed for the weekends and holidays, when she could spend hours roaming the hills and fields surrounding the Birches.

Jane continued to learn valuable lessons about animal life. One dog, named Rusty, was especially influential. Many people believe that animals sim-

Jane Goodall: Animal Behaviorist and Writer

ply react to the world around them. When a dog is ordered to sit, it sits. When food is placed before it, it eats. When it is tired, it sleeps.

But when Jane threw a ball out the window, she watched in fascination as Rusty looked to see where it landed, ran downstairs, barked to have a door opened, and then retrieved the ball. To Jane, Rusty had not simply reacted to events, he had made a plan. Rusty's action suggested a far greater intelligence than most humans believed possible.

Rusty also taught Jane a lesson on the emotional intelligence of animals. When Jane scolded Rusty for pushing a door open with muddy paws, he acted hurt and angry. Before, when his paws were clean, Jane had praised him for opening the same door. Rusty seemed to feel that he was a victim of injustice, and he sat facing the wall, ignoring Jane until she leaned down and apologized. Jane described Rusty's reaction as "sulking"—a very human emotion.

Germany and London

At age eighteen, Jane graduated from a private school at Parkstone, near Bournemouth. Jane hoped to continue her education at a college, but she needed a scholarship to pay the tuition. Unfortunately, she had struggled to learn foreign languages, and the top universities required her to improve her grades.

In part to improve her ability to speak German, Jane spent four months in Germany, a country still recovering from the ravages of World War II. But the German family members she stayed with were keen to improve their English, and they refused to speak German. So Jane learned very little.

Vanne also hoped that Jane would learn that not all Germans were evil, despite the bitterness that still existed in Europe for the atrocities committed by the Nazis in World War II. When Jane was in the German city of Cologne, she saw the spires of that city's magnificent cathedral. Allied bombings had destroyed much of the city, but the cathedral—blackened by flames—still stood. The image affected Jane powerfully. Despite Hitler and the destruction of war, the cathedral endured, a symbol that good eventually prevails over evil.

When Jane returned to England, Vanne suggested that Jane study to become a secretary. After all, said Vanne, secretaries can get jobs anywhere in the world. Jane, still dreaming that she could work with animals in Africa, agreed.

Jane went to London to enter a secretarial

school. There, she enjoyed the pleasures of the city—the museums, the art galleries, and the exciting nightlife.

After receiving her secretarial diploma, Jane went to work at her aunt's clinic. The clinic helped children crippled by accident or disease. Jane wrote down the comments from doctors on each case and then typed them up. She learned of tiny infants crippled by club feet, children confined to wheelchairs, and teenagers dying of muscular dystrophy.

"My months at the clinic," wrote Jane in *Reason for Hope*, "taught me a great deal about human resilience, both physical and mental; and made me appreciate my own extraordinarily healthy body. I know how lucky I am, and I do not, not ever, take it for granted."

Jane left the clinic to work at Oxford University—a school she hoped to attend someday. But for now, she spent hours doing boring office work. She soon left that job and returned to London, where she found work making music selections for documentary films, a task she loved.

Still, her dream to go to Africa lived on, and on December 18, 1956, she received a letter that changed her life. The letter came from an old school friend, Marie Claude Mange—nicknamed Clo. Clo wrote that her parents had bought a farm in Kenya, Africa. Would Jane come to visit? Filled with excitement, Jane responded yes.

Jane returned to Bournemouth. There, she could find a job and save the money for the fare without the expensive distractions of life in London.

She became a waitress. Each weekend, Jane stowed her earnings away, under a carpet in the drawing room. Five months later, the family entered the room, drew the curtains, and took the money out from under the carpet. While the others looked on, Jane counted the total. It was enough to buy her a round-trip ticket. Jane was going to Africa.

AFRICA 2

Jane Goodall, now twenty-three, boarded the passenger liner *Kenya Castle* in London and waved a tearful good-bye to her family and friends. The liner's engines pushed the boat out to sea. London, England, and her old life disappeared over the horizon. "The adventure, the voyage to Tarzan's Africa, to the land of lions, leopards, elephants, giraffes, and monkeys, had actually begun," remembered Goodall in *Reason for Hope*.

The trip to Africa filled Jane with emotion—fear, excitement, and wonder. While her

The port of Mombasa. This was Goodall's first view of Africa.

roommates huddled below in their cabin during a storm, Jane stayed on deck, thrilled by the whipping wind and the bubbling ocean spray. And, as always, Jane was thrilled to glimpse wildlife—a school of dolphins or a shark's triangular fin slicing through the water.

In three weeks, the *Kenya Castle* traveled down the west coast of Africa, around the tip of that great continent, and up the east coast to the port city of Mombasa. There, Goodall left the ship and boarded

Jane Goodall: Animal Behaviorist and Writer

a train for the two-day journey to Nairobi, the capital city of Kenya.

Goodall spent three magical weeks with Clo and her family. She examined the paw print of a giant leopard, listened to unfamiliar birdcalls, and took part in a hunt—the last one, she vowed shortly afterwards.

Unwilling to be a burden upon Clo's generosity, Goodall went to Nairobi, leased an apartment, and became a secretary in a British company. The work was dull, but it paid the bills and Goodall was convinced that an opportunity to work closely with animals would soon appear.

It did. One night after a dinner party, another guest heard about Goodall's interest in wildlife. "If you're interested in animals," the guest said, "you should meet Louis Leakey."

Louis Leakey

Leakey was a famous anthropologist and paleontologist—a scientist who studies ancient wildlife by examining their bones and fossils. He worked at the Coryndon Museum of Natural History in Nairobi.

Goodall visited Leakey's office, a space littered with bones, fossils, and ancient artifacts. Leakey, then fifty-four, had a striking appearance, with a shock of white hair that hung shaggily from his head. He took Goodall around the museum, peppering her with questions about various exhibits. Goodall had been studying African wildlife for more than a year, and she could answer most of them. When she didn't know an answer, she at least understood the meaning of the question.

Leakey's extensive knowledge of Africa and its people enchanted Goodall. Leakey, in turn, was

Louis Leakey. This famous anthropologist played a vital role in Goodall's career.

impressed by Goodall's youthful enthusiasm, intelligence, and motivation. Despite having no experience in a university, Goodall demonstrated a tremendous knowledge of animals. Leakey saw something special in the young woman. He offered her a job as his personal secretary.

For the next year, Goodall learned about the animal life and culture of East Africa. In 1957, Leakey invited Goodall and Gillian Trace, another English woman at the museum, to accompany him and his wife on their annual dig at Olduvai Gorge in Tanganyika (now called Tanzania).

Olduvai was located on the vast plains of the Serengeti, which at that time had no roads and very few people. To find the gorge, Leakey had to search for the tire tracks he had left in the long grass on last year's dig.

Leakey had discovered several ancient tools in the area, and he was convinced that apelike humans had made and used them thousands of years ago. At that time, most of the world believed humans had first emerged in Europe or Asia. Leakey, however, was convinced that Africa was the spot. He was determined to find a fossil or bone of humankind's ancestors and prove his theory correct.

Leakey's colleagues in England scoffed at his plan. But Leakey, a brilliant and energetic scientist, was undeterred. Goodall described him as a genius who spoke in rapid sentences and jumped from one conclusion to the next. He often relied upon instinct and unconventional reasoning—alienating concepts to a scientific world that prized fact and objectivity. The group's work in the Olduvai Gorge was based on Leakey's calculated hunch that somewhere in the earth there lay the evidence he sought.

For Goodall, the dig was a dream come true. During the day, she used a knife to chop at the hard soil, occasionally turning up the fossil of an ancient animal.

"I would be filled with awe by the sight or the feel of some bone I held in my hand," she wrote in her book *In the Shadow of Man*. "This—this very bone—had once been part of a living breathing animal that had walked and slept and propagated [reproduced] its species. What had it really looked like? What color was its hair; what was the odor of its body?"

At night, Goodall rested by the fire and listened to the distant growls of a lion or the high-pitched cackle of a hyena. The conversation among Leakey, his wife, Goodall, and Trace flowed back and forth, touching on various subjects—the finds of the day, the habits of ancient man, the mystery of God and the universe.

At the end of the three-month dig, Leakey wondered aloud about the habits of the great apes and chimpanzees—animals that lived in central Africa. These creatures were the closest living relatives to humans, and Leakey theorized that the great apes might behave in a similar manner to Stone Age man. He was eager to begin a study.

The dig ended, and the group returned to Nairobi and the natural history museum. Goodall was growing impatient with her work. She loved to study animals, but she grew increasingly horrified at the idea of trapping and killing creatures to use as specimens. Goodall understood that specimens were needed for study. But why so many?

Goodall was tired of examining lifeless, stiff animals displayed in exhibits. She wanted to study living, breathing animals in their own habitats. While Goodall boiled with impatience, Leakey continued to discuss his plan of observing chimpanzees in the wild.

Finally, Goodall spoke her mind. "Louis, I wish you wouldn't keep talking about it because that's just what I want to do," she said.

To Leakey, they were the words he had been waiting to hear. "Jane," he answered, "I've been waiting for you to tell me that. Why on earth did you think I talked about those chimpanzees with you?"

Goodall was stunned and overwhelmed at his proposal. How could she, just a young woman, enter the wilds of Africa and conduct a scientific project that had never been attempted before?

Leakey quickly reassured her. For his bold new study, Leakey wanted a fresh, enthusiastic, and intelligent person. He was actually pleased that Goodall had not been trained in a formal university. Leakey was proposing a new way of looking at the world, and he needed a person who was capable of seeing it. "When he put it like that," Goodall later wrote in *Reason for Hope*, "I had to admit that I was the perfect choice!"

Preparations

Flushed with enthusiasm, Goodall was ready to plunge into the jungle immediately. But Leakey still had to raise money and receive permission for the experiments. It would take months.

In the meantime, Goodall returned to England. She read everything she could about chimpanzees, and she discovered that few people had studied them in their habitat. In 1923, Dr. Henry W. Nissen searched for chimpanzees in French Guinea. For two and a half months, he tried to track the animals, but he did little except record some observations and then shoot the specimens for analysis.

In another study, two psychologists observed the behavior of a colony of chimpanzees in captivity. Goodall was fascinated by their conclusions, and she went to the London Zoo to observe two chimpanzees. But the chimps sat listlessly in concrete cells, cut off from other animals and diversion of any kind. One chimp appeared to be insane. He sat hunched in a corner of his cell and seemed to count his fingers over and over for hours. Goodall, shocked by his appearance, vowed to help him someday.

Leakey had to convince a skeptical scientific community that this study was possible. When they heard that Leakey planned to send a young woman into the jungle, many believed that the old man had finally gone nuts. But Leakey was persistent, and he secured funding for the project from the Wilkie Foundation in Des Plaines, Illinois. The money provided a small boat, a tent, airfare, and enough supplies to keep Goodall in the field for six months.

The site was the Gombe Stream Chimpanzee Reserve in what is now Tanzania, a country in southeastern Africa. This reserve consists of a 20-square-mile (52-square-kilometer) area set aside for animals on the coast of Lake Tanganyika.

Another hurdle appeared. Leakey and Goodall were not concerned about Jane living alone in a vast forest. Government officials, however, balked. No

Gombe. This area of Tanzania would become a second home to Goodall during her many years of research.

Jane Goodall: Animal Behaviorist and Writer

way, they said, would they allow a young white woman to enter the jungle alone. Leakey argued relentlessly and finally the authorities agreed, but only if Goodall took a companion. Goodall turned to her mother, Vanne. It was settled.

After Goodall and her mother flew to Nairobi, Leakey received a telegram from the district commissioner. A quarrel had broken out among African fisherman over who had the rights to fish from the beaches of Gombe. Until the issue was settled, Vanne and Goodall would have to stay put.

Though bitterly disappointed, Goodall took Leakey's suggestion that she go to Lolui Island on Lake Victoria. The island was home to a population of vervet monkeys. They were smaller than chimpanzees, but Goodall could practice her observation techniques there.

For three weeks, Goodall observed the monkeys and gained valuable knowledge. She learned what kinds of clothing to wear and how to move without frightening the animals. When she finally received a note telling her to return to Nairobi, Goodall left with some reluctance, since she had learned so much about the vervet monkeys.

The fishing rights issue at Gombe had been

settled, and Vanne and Goodall loaded up a Land Rover for the 800-mile (1,287-kilometer) trip to the town of Kigoma, just across Lake Tanganyika from Gombe Stream Game Reserve. The driver, Bernard Verdcourt, was a botanist at the Coryndon Museum.

A vervet monkey. Goodall spent time observing this kind of primate before she went to Gombe.

But Vanne and Goodall were again delayed. Just 25 miles (40 km) to the west, the people of the Congo were revolting against their European leaders. Belgian refugees streamed over the border as the countryside exploded into violence. Vanne, Goodall, and Verdcourt helped make sandwiches and hand out cigarettes, chocolate, and fruit to crowds of hungry, despondent refugees. The hotels were crammed with people. Others took shelter in warehouses. But even after the refugees moved on two days later, the game ranger of the reserve refused to allow Vanne and Goodall to enter Gombe until the situation stabilized.

They waited another week and permission finally came. They loaded their gear onto a government boat piloted by the Ranger David Anstey and set out onto the waters of Lake Tanganyika for the 12-mile (19-km) journey to Gombe.

Goodall expected the study to last maybe two years. Leakey predicted that she would need ten. Verdcourt bid the pair farewell and wondered if he would ever see them again.

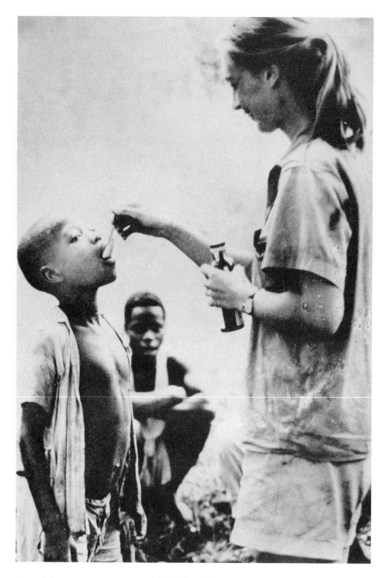

In Africa. At times, Goodall helped her mother give medicine to the native people.

GOMBE

3

As the launch churned north through the lake waters, Goodall scanned the coastline. Rocky outcroppings jutted into the water, forming a series of bays. Hills rose rapidly to 2,500 feet (763 m). Patches of forest nestled in the valleys that were carved out by fast-moving streams rushing into the lake. Most of the forest had been chopped down. Here and there, Jane spotted small clusters of mud-and-grass huts built by fishermen and their families.

After traveling about 7 miles (11 km), the launch reached the southern border of the game reserve. In this protected region, the mountains bristled with trees and the valleys were choked with thick forest. Gazing at the forbidding region, Vanne wondered how anyone could cross these steep slopes and travel through the dense vegetation, but she kept these thoughts to herself. Anstey silently predicted that Goodall would last six weeks.

Vanne, Goodall, and their cook, Dominic, spent that night in camp near the headquarters of two government game scouts. Many of the local Africans were disturbed by the presence of Goodall. Unable to understand why a woman would come to the forest to watch monkeys, they suspected she was a government spy.

Goodall grew discouraged when she learned that Anstey insisted she be accompanied at all times. But, Anstey had his reasons. One companion, a chief's son from a local fishing village, would make sure that Goodall didn't falsely report the number of chimps she saw. Many of the Africans, wanting the park to revert back to public land, hoped she would find nothing.

Another reason was Goodall's safety. Anstey didn't want Goodall to be injured and alone if she tumbled down one of the park's treacherous slopes.

Animal attack was also a serious danger. Just two days after arriving in Gombe, a fisherman took Goodall to a tree trunk splintered and gouged by the horns of an African buffalo. The huge beast had chased another fisherman, forcing him to clamber up the tree to safety. The buffalo had battered the trunk with its horns for more than an hour before finally leaving.

Despite this evidence of danger in the forest, Goodall still hoped to work alone. She believed that the chimps would find a group of humans too threatening, and they would flee.

Into the Jungle

In her book, *In the Shadow of Man*, Goodall described how her two guides, Adolf and Rashidi, took her into the Gombe forest for the first time. Pressing into the dense underbrush, the trees forming a canopy 100 feet (31 m) overhead, Goodall watched as a bird glided by, followed by a pack of redtail monkeys darting from branch to branch.

After hiking for less than an hour, Adolf halted by a large tree hung with clusters of fruits. Partially eaten fruit was strewn on the ground below. The tree, called msulula, was a favorite eating spot for the chimpanzees. Hoping that they would soon return, Goodall and her two guides walked for to a grassy spot opposite the tree and settled down to wait.

Suddenly, a low, hooting sound filled the forest. As the sound grew louder, more hoots joined in. The voices blended together and then broke again into high-pitched screams. A group of chimpanzees was approaching the msulula.

Rashidi alerted Goodall. A shadowy figure was climbing up the tree, followed by another, and another, and another—for a total of sixteen. One figure carried a small infant. For the next two hours, Goodall watched dark, fur-covered arms reach out to the grab the fruit and disappear again. Then the figures climbed down the tree and silently vanished into the forest.

For the next ten days, Goodall watched chimps feeding in the msulula tree. But she soon grew frustrated. She could watch some groups interacting, but following individual chimps and observing them closely proved impossible. The msulala's leaves were too dense, and when Goodall attempted to get closer, the chimps fled, terrified of this strange, hairless "white ape."

When the fruit season ended, the chimps stopped visiting the msulala. For eight difficult weeks, Goodall searched for them. Rising every day at dawn, she said good-bye to Vanne and hiked with her guides into the reserve. Goodall avoided the thick forest, where chimps could easily hear her scrambling through the brush. But on the open grassy ridges, she could only catch a glimpse of them. Even from hundreds of yards away, the chimps fled. She stayed out until the sun had dipped low in the sky and settled in the west.

Vanne's Medical Clinic

While her daughter roamed the forests of Gombe, Vanne had opened a medical clinic. Many Africans, curious about the white women, visited the camp. Vanne owned only a first aid kit, but she attempted to cure any of the small ailments plaguing the Africans. Once, a man showed up in camp with two giant sores festering in his lower leg. When he refused to go to the hospital, Vanne told him to use a home remedy. Twice a day, she said, he should drip saltwater over the sores. After three weeks, the swelling had receded and the sores healed.

Vanne's reputation as a medicine woman spread

Medicine woman. Vanne was eager to help the Africans, and soon they came to trust her.

quickly, and soon villagers crowded the campsite. Vanne's work proved invaluable to Goodall. Many Africans had still been suspicious of the two Englishwomen, but Vanne's actions dispelled their hostility and established trust.

The Peak

After three months, Goodall had seen very little of the chimps, and the money that funded the study was running out. Worse, Vanne and Goodall grew feverish and weak due to malaria—despite a doctor's assurances that malaria didn't exist in the region.

Goodall and Vanne stayed in their tent, sweltering and burning with fever. Vanne grew so delirious that she wandered from her bed and was later found by Dominic, who returned her safely to the tent.

Hours in the field. In spite of illness, Goodall worked long days while she observed the chimpanzees of Gombe.

Dominic urged them to visit a doctor, but Goodall protested that they were too ill to make the three-hour trip.

When Goodall's fever finally broke, she eagerly went back to work. But she was still weak. Unwilling to allow the guides to see her looking so distressed, she left camp alone one morning. She struggled up a nearby mountain and discovered an excellent viewing spot of the valley.

Goodall spotted three chimps on a ravine no more than 80 yards (731 m) away. Instead of fleeing, they watched her closely before moving on calmly and vanishing into the forest. Hours later, another group crossed the ridge. Again, they stared at her but did not panic. They descended to some fig trees below and were soon feeding in delight.

"That day, in fact, marked the turning point in my study," wrote Goodall in *In the Shadow of Man*. The chimps were finally recognizing that the "white ape" was not a threat.

For several weeks, Goodall returned to her solitary spot on the mountain, or the Peak as she called it, and watched the chimps feasting on figs. The Peak was critical to her study. Besides providing an superb observation point, it allowed the chimps to get used to Goodall from a safe distance. Goodall always wore the same brown-colored clothing and never attempted to follow the chimps.

Goodall's guides also stopped shadowing her every movement. Knowing that she spent her time at the Peak, they checked on her only once a day. Goodall no longer resented the guides, because they had taught her a great deal about the forest and the animals in it.

From the Peak, Goodall caught more fascinating pictures of chimp life. She watched as they wove nests out of branches high in the trees for sleeping, even preparing a bushel of soft leaves as a pillow. She saw one figure greet another with reassuring gestures very similar to hugs and kisses. She watched young chimpanzees jump onto a bouncy branch and swing to the ground, over and over again.

She returned to her camp every night and transcribed to a journal the observations she had scribbled in a notebook. By this time, Goodall could recognize individual chimps, and she gave them names. One ancient female, she called Flo. Her infant daughter was Fifi and her young son was Figan. David Graybeard was a calm, handsome male with a white beard.

Fifi and Ferdinand. Goodall related to the chimps so well that she gave them names.

Discoveries

Within a few months, as she described in *In the Shadow of Man*, Goodall made a breakthrough discovery. She was watching David Graybeard resting in a tree and chewing on food. A female and a young chimpanzee sat nearby, begging to share in the meal. Graybeard spit some of it—a reddish-colored substance—into their hands. Goodall realized with shock that the chimps were eating the flesh of a pig.

Until then, the scientific community believed that chimps ate mostly plants and insects. Only men, they thought, hunted large animals and shared the meat among themselves. Goodall's discovery blurred the traditional line between human and chimpanzee.

Goodall made her second great discovery on another day, when she spotted David Graybeard hunched over a large mound of red earth—a termite nest. Goodall watched as David poked a long blade of grass into the mound and withdrew it. The blade was covered with white, fat termites. David plucked off the juicy termites with his tongue and teeth, munched them, and then put the blade into the mound again. He pulled out another swarm of bristling insects and ate them with relish. Goodall was stunned. David was doing more than just manipulating the grass, he was using it as a tool. Until that moment, it was thought that only humans used tools. After all, tools separated humans from animals.

Goodall watched as David carefully pulled up another blade of grass, trimmed it to the proper length, and resumed his feasting. Later, she telegraphed Leakey and described her observations.

"I feel that scientists holding to this definition are faced with three choices: They must accept chimpanzees as man, by definition, they must redefine man; or they must redefine tools," telegraphed the jubilant Leakey back to Goodall.

Goodall's discovery spread around the world, making old theories of mankind suddenly outdated. Scientists and anthropologists argued furiously over the conclusions. Some refused to believe it at all, charging that Goodall must have taught the chimps how to use the tools.

Others were impressed. One group—the National Geographic Society—decided to fund another year of Goodall and Leakey's research.

CLOSE ENCOUNTERS

After spending about five months in Africa, Vanne had to return to England. Goodall was left alone with Dominic and another helper, Hassan. But by then, Goodall had become used to Gombe, and the goodwill established by Vanne with the local residents helped her immeasurably.

Goodall was also drawing closer and closer to the chimpanzees. The wet season came to Gombe, when thundering downpours could last for several hours. While the constant rain often kept Goodall chilly and miserable, it also allowed to her to get closer

Midday rest. Flo and Flint built this nest high up in the tree branches.

Jane Goodall: Animal Behaviorist and Writer

to the chimps. The forest floor, once covered in dry, brittle leaves, was now soggy and wet. Goodall's movements were faster and quieter, and the chimps were distracted by their own attempts to keep warm.

One morning, Goodall wrote in *In the Shadow of Man*, she heard a group of chimps and began to move toward them. A curtain of rain dropped over the forest, forcing Goodall to stop. When it finally let up, Goodall hurried on, the leaves around her dripping with raindrops and the bark of trees dark with moisture.

Suddenly she spied a dark, hunched figure just yards ahead. Goodall stopped and squatted on the ground. The chimp, not seeing her, didn't move. Goodall waited in the drizzle when a soft "hoo" sounded to her right. Goodall recognized the call—the worried cry of a nervous chimp. Slowly and carefully, she turned her head in the direction of the sound. She saw nothing. When she again looked ahead, the figure had vanished.

Goodall heard a noise and looked up. A large male chimp loomed, staring at her intensely. Goodall quickly glanced away. Making eye contact for too long could be taken as a threat, and Goodall would have no chance fighting with an enraged chimpanzee.

Another rustling sound came from her left. Goodall looked and saw another chimp.

The chimp above her let out a long scream and violently shook the branch. It was a threat. The other chimps made the same sound, blasting the forest with their ferocious cries.

Despite the fear that surged up within her, Goodall tried to look preoccupied by scraping for some roots in the ground. Again, the chimp savagely shook the branch, this time hitting her. Another chimp rushed out of the undergrowth directly at Goodall. She crouched over and veered off into the jungle.

It took several minutes before Goodall realized that she was alone once again. She felt both terrified and exhilarated, she wrote in *In the Shadow of Man*.

Weeks later, Goodall sat a short distance from a fruit tree, where she hoped the chimps would soon arrive to feed. They did, but not from the direction she expected. Behind her, she heard the footsteps of approaching chimps. Hoping not to frighten them, Goodall lay down. She expected the chimps to pass by and begin feeding. They came closer and then suddenly stopped. A chimp retreated quickly and uttered a sharp yell.

Another chimp clambered into a nearby tree, looked down at Goodall, and screamed at her. After a few moments, he began to descend the tree and approach Goodall, his lips pulled back over his yellow teeth with rage. Now he shook a branch, then slapped a tree, then shook a branch again, screaming. The dark figure jumped from the tree and went behind Goodall. He barked, stamped his feet, and then slapped her hard across the head.

Now Goodall sat up. The chimp stared at her, and Goodall feared that he would attack. But he stopped, and walked away, glancing over his shoulder as he disappeared into the forest.

"There was a sense of triumph," wrote Goodall about the encounter in *In the Shadow of Man*. "I had made real contact with a wild chimpanzee—or perhaps it should be the other way around."

Contact

Over the next few months, Goodall was again frustrated. The sun heated the lush, moist forest, turning the area into a vast sauna that sapped her body of energy. Her fevers returned, and the humidity was so thick that she sometimes climbed into the upper branches of a tree for relief. In addition, the chimps had broken into smaller groups and were difficult to track.

But as the season changed, strong winds cleared the valleys of the oppressive humidity, and the fig tree again hung heavy with fruit. Goodall could now leave the Peak and get much closer to the chimps, though they still treated her with confusion and fear. After another fruitless day of searching for the chimps, Goodall climbed to the Peak and settled down, hoping to watch a chimp build a nest before darkness fell scarcely two hours later. Then she spotted four chimps feeding in a fig tree. Hoping to get closer, she left the Peak.

She made her way quietly through the forest and reached her vantage point, but by that time, the chimps had heard her and disappeared. As she lowered her eyes from the empty branches in disappointment, she realized that she was being watched. Less than 20 yards (18 m) away, two males sat staring at her. Goodall waited for them to panic, to scream, and to run. But they didn't. Slowly, Goodall sat down. The two males continued to look at her intently and then stopped. They turned their attention to themselves and began searching each other's fur for dirt, a common process called grooming.

"Without doubt, this was the proudest moment I had known," wrote Goodall in *In the Shadow of Man*. "I had been accepted by the two magnificent creatures grooming each other in front of me."

Everyday events. Goodall often watched while chimpanzees groomed one another.

This acceptance was the first in history. After a year of unbelievable persistence, Goodall had done something no other human being had ever done—observed wild chimpanzees on their own terms. The National Geographic Society was eager to send a photographer to Gombe and photograph Goodall's work. But Goodall hesitated. She was worried that a new person would shatter the trust she had worked so hard to build with the chimpanzees. Instead, Goodall suggested that they send her sister, Judy. Judy looked a lot like Goodall, and Goodall hoped that the chimps would accept her readily. The National Geographic Society refused to finance an inexperienced photographer, but *Reveille*, a British newspaper, decided to take the chance.

Unfortunately for Judy, the weather was miserable during her stay in Gombe. She hunched under a plastic tarp, tried to keep her clumsy equipment dry, and waited for chimps that rarely appeared. When they did show up, the rain was often so heavy that it made taking pictures impossible. However, Judy did take some wonderful pictures of camp life and enough images of the chimpanzees to satisfy the newspaper.

Cambridge

When Judy returned to England in December 1961, Jane Goodall went with her. Louis Leakey had convinced Cambridge University, one of the world's most prestigious universities, to allow Goodall to bypass the undergraduate degree and work for a Ph.D. in ethology—the study of animal behavior. Goodall's work at Gombe would be her thesis.

But leaving Gombe, even for just a few months of class, was difficult for Goodall. She had grown to love the individual chimpanzees, and she was concerned that her absence would wipe out her accomplishments of the past eighteen months. Still, she recognized the opportunity of formal learning provided by Cambridge, and when she left Africa, she took 850 pages of chimpanzee observations with her. She had no idea that her study would provoke a firestorm of controversy.

A growing bond. During her time in Gombe, Goodall earned the confidence of the chimpanzees she studied.

THE WORLD NOTICES

In the 1950s and 1960s, the science of ethology was working hard for respect from the scientific community. Through the 1800s and 1900s, ethology was a compilation of hours of observation. Konrad Lorenz, the founder of ethology, became famous by spending hours observing the actions of animals. He did not experiment with them; he simply observed and recorded what he saw.

But that was the problem. Even when they are looking at the same object, people often see completely different things. One person can see the sleek movements of a snake and describe it as fleeing. Another can find them threatening and sinister. Is the snake acting afraid—or aggressive? Who is right? It's difficult to know for sure, and that's what bothered ethologists, who were trying create firm rules about animal behavior through exact science.

Goodall described the chimpanzees of Gombe in colorful language. She created portraits of personalities and even gave chimps names. Goodall was suggesting that empathy and intuition can be effective and helpful tools in observing animals, as long as the observer is precise and disciplined. Many ethologists were horrified. In their opinion, Goodall was taking the whole science backward. It is no surprise that Goodall clashed with many of her professors at Cambridge.

The chimpanzee is more like humans than any other living animal. The DNA difference between humans and chimps is around 1 percent. But it was one thing to say that chimps and humans have the same nervous system. It was quite another thing to suggest that chimps feel pain, joy, fear, anger, and a thousand different shades of emotions, just like humans.

Ethologists preferred to make "scientific" observations of animals. And being "scientific" meant being cold, rational, and unemotional. Goodall, however, presented the chimps as being passionate, jealous, resourceful, and cunning—as problem solvers and tool users. The ethologists scoffed. Goodall was describing the chimps as human.

Her sin was unforgivable. Goodall once gave a lecture about a chimp named Figan to a hall filled with ethologists. Figan, said Goodall, was an adolescent who was still learning. Once, a crowd of monkeys entered Goodall's camp, ate a meal of bananas, and left. Figan, however, stayed behind, and Goodall gave him another bunch of bananas. Figan screamed with pleasure. The other males heard him, rushed back, and took the bananas. The next time, Goodall again gave Figan a bunch of bananas after the other chimps had moved on. Again, Figan was delighted, but this time he kept his cries muffled in his throat, obviously not wanting to repeat his mistake. Figan soon enjoyed his bananas alone.

Goodall expected the ethologists to be excited about this obvious sign of intelligence. But instead she was met with a silence. Goodall's account was an anecdote—a story. It was hardly a fact, and facts were the basis of scientific study. "Looking back," wrote Goodall in her book *Through a Window*, "I suspected that everyone was interested, but it was, of course, not permissible to present a mere 'anecdote' as evidence for anything."

Goodall encountered the same attitude when she submitted a paper describing her observations to *Annals of the New York Academy of Science*, a scientific journal. Her manuscript came back with all her

Spending time together. Goodall tried to understand the emotions of the animals she observed.

mentions of "he" and "she" crossed out and replaced with "it." To the editor, only a human could be a "he" or a "she." A chimp was a mere animal—a "thing." Furious, Goodall, crossed out all the "its" and replaced them with their original gender.

Goodall was also one of the few women in a field dominated by men. Almost all of her professors were male, and eventually, some writers would attribute Goodall's revolutionary perspective to the fact that she is a female. But Goodall would later say that she was simply being logical.

"I didn't give two hoots for what they thought," Goodall said in Sy Montgomery's *Walking with the Great Apes*. "They were wrong, I was right. That's why I was lucky that I was never going into these things for science. And I didn't care about the Ph.D., it didn't matter. I would listen, I just wouldn't do what they said. Then I would go back to what I was doing at Gombe."

RETURN TO GOMBE

Goodall returned to Gombe, fearful that the chimps may have forgotten her. But to her delight, they seemed to be even more relaxed in her presence than they were when she left.

When Goodall returned to camp after a day at the Peak, Dominic was bursting with excitement. He said that a chimp had fed in a tree in the center of the camp. After a meal of oil nuts, the chimp had walked over to Goodall's tent and helped himself to a bushel of bananas set out for Goodall's dinner.

Graybeard visited camp three more times that week, each time being rewarded with bananas. He visited again later that month and even took a banana from Goodall's hand. She was stunned with happiness. From then on, when Graybeard spotted Goodall in the forest, he walked over and checked her pocket for a banana. The other chimps stared in amazement. Their fear of Goodall was fading fast.

Chimps on Film

In 1962, a National Geographic Society photographer named Hugo van Lawick arrived at Gombe. A Dutch baron, van Lawick had worked with Leakey at Olduvai Gorge. Leakey was so impressed with van Lawick's work and his love of animals that he recommended him to the National Geographic as the perfect person to capture Goodall's work on film.

Leakey also sent a note to Goodall's mother with a different theme. Van Lawick, said Leakey, would make a perfect husband for Goodall.

Van Lawick arrived in Gombe and set up his cameras on giant tripods. On his first day, he hid in a tent and waited for David Graybeard to arrive for his daily meal of bananas. The clever chimp soon noticed that something was different. He finished

Captured on film. Photographer Hugo van Lawick joined Goodall and her work in Gombe.

eating and walked over to van Lawick's tent. He suddenly pulled up the tent flap and stared at the camera. That was all. He returned to his eating. Van Lawick was soon accepted by the other chimps of Gombe, and his films captured the stunning world of chimpanzees.

By the time van Lawick left Gombe, he had

filmed chimps grooming each other and eating the carcass of a colobus monkey. In another series, van Lawick captured Graybeard as he hunted for termites with a stalk of grass.

These images, published in *National Geographic*, made Goodall known all over the world. In fact, the first article, "My Life Among the Wild Chimpanzees," sold out, forcing *National Geographic* to make another printing. Goodall received the National Geographic Society's Franklin Burr Award for Contribution to Science in 1963 and 1964.

But if Goodall's work was applauded in many corners, others were disturbed by the casual interaction between humans and animals. Louis Leakey was especially incensed that Goodall was offering the chimps bananas. The animals, he said, would raid other villages for food, which would lead to a campaign of extermination. Worse, chimps were much stronger than humans. If a chimp discovered how easy it was to kill a human, it could lead to disaster.

Scientists also debated how much humans should interact with animal subjects. They criticized Jane, saying that the bananas changed the way the chimps acted and therefore her observations should be disregarded.

Working marriage. Goodall and van Lawick found their love of animals to be a bond between them.

Marriage and Family

In van Lawick, Goodall saw a soul mate. His work ethic was as strong as hers, and he loved the animals with a passion that matched her own. After van Lawick returned to England, he sent Goodall a telegram asking her to marry him. She said yes.

Next spring, March 1964, the proud couple was married in England. At the reception, their wedding cake was topped with a clay figurine of David Graybeard and the walls were hung with huge colored portraits of Flo, Fifi, David Graybeard, Goliath, and other chimpanzees.

On their honeymoon, the couple learned that Flo had given birth to another baby. Cutting their vacation to three days, the couple quickly returned to Africa for the opportunity to observe a baby chimp.

Three years later, Goodall gave birth to her own son, Hugo Eric Louis, nicknamed Grub. She would later write that her own experience of motherhood helped teach her about the chimpanzees she observed every day.

For the next decade Goodall, van Lawick, and their student researchers would make stunning observations of chimpanzee life.

Mutual interest. This chimpanzee appears to be as curious about Goodall as she was of him.

THE CHIMPANZEES OF GOMBE

The chimpanzees of Gombe were Jane Goodall's "people of the forest." To the untrained observer, they spend most of their time eating, in search of food, or sleeping. Then suddenly, they disappear, hustling over the forest floor on all fours or leaping from branch to branch. They are powerful, at least twice as strong as humans, and they may live to be more than fifty years old.

Goodall spent much of her time observing the family she had initially named. The mother, Flo, had three children. Chimps usually nurse on their mother's milk for more than four years and are weaned by the age of five. The oldest son, Faben, was now a teenager and spent much of his time away from the family and hanging out with older males. Faben's younger brother, Figan, also wanted to be with the males but was still too young. Instead, he hung around Flo and his younger sister, Fifi.

The Contest for Alpha Male

The chimpanzees of Gombe numbered about fifty, though they moved about in smaller groups. The groups reassembled at various times during the year, usually when the fig trees swelled with fruit.

When this occurred, a contest began among the males to demonstrate who was the alpha male—the leader of the group. Goodall remembers observing one such contest.

With hoots, screams, and hollers, the males scrambled up and down a hillside, shaking bushes, throwing rocks, snapping branches from trees and dragging them along the ground before hurling them in a display of power. Their hair bristled upright, their brows drew together, and their mouths formed a grim frown—not unlike an angry human face.

While the females hid, the male chimps swung through trees and raced about, but they rarely made contact with each other. The noise and bluster was a calculated attempt to intimidate the other chimps. A serious fight could lead to injury and infection, and it rarely came to that.

After fifteen minutes, the lead male had emerged victorious, and the other chimps gathered around to make gestures of submission. One male made a short bow. Another offered a kiss. An infant, terrified by the noise, clambered up to the alpha male, who gave him a reassuring pat on the back. Slowly, peace returned, and the chimps joined together to groom each other, a process that always calmed everyone's nerves.

Figan, who had watched the display, gently shook a tree as if to try out his strength. The other males ignored him. Figan was an awkward adolescent, bored with his younger sister and Flo but not yet accepted by the older males.

As Figan watched the males, he decided to give it a try. He shook a tree and raced into an open field. But the other males had stopped and were looking at him with hard stares. Showing off was unacceptable from an adolescent. Realizing that he had overstepped his bounds, Figan turned his display into a series of somersaults, as if he had been playing all along. Though still young, Figan was showing signs that he wanted to be the alpha male one day.

Flo gave birth to another son called Flint. Chimpanzees have babies about once every five or six years, so the new member of the group attracted a lot of attention. Fifi, a young female just five years old, was fascinated.

While Figan acted bored, Fifi hovered over Flo, trying to pry the infant from her arms and hold him herself. But Flo would not risk giving the infant to the young Fifi, and she tried to distract her young daughter by tickling her. When this failed, Flo finally walked away, leaving Fifi frustrated and with her lips drawn into a pout.

Mother and Son

The bond between an infant chimp and his or her mother can be incredibly powerful. For the first six months, Flint always stayed at his mother's side, either clinging to the fur beneath her or, more often, riding on Flo's back like a jockey on a horse.

Flint was a demanding son. By this time, Flo was old, and she didn't have the energy to resist his temper tantrums. Protected by his powerful family, Flint often tried to intimidate other members of the group, though this sometimes earned him a slap for his impudence. When he got angry, Flo didn't push him away, but instead tried to distract him and reassure him until his rage had passed.

This changed when Flint was five and Flo gave birth to a daughter, Flame. Flint was stunned by the

A motherly hug. Goodall developed an important relationship with the chimps she encountered.

new arrival, and then he grew enraged, slapping and screaming at Flo when she refused to nurse him. When Flame died after a few months, Flint was thrilled—he was once again the baby of the family.

Flint's world came crashing down around him when Flo finally died. He found her in a stream, and he poked her lifeless body in confusion and brushed away the swarming clouds of flies. He grew depressed and sullen. When he finally seemed to understand that she was no longer alive, Flint built a nest overlooking the stream and stayed there. The rest of the group moved on. After three weeks of bitter mourning, Flint joined his mother in death.

Figan on Top

Despite the tragedy, Flo's family continued to prosper. Fifi had become a mother herself and her brother Figan had at last realized his dream of becoming alpha male. Becoming alpha male—and holding the position—is very demanding. It took more than sheer strength; it took cunning and the ability to make and break alliances.

The alpha male before Figan was Mike. He ruled the group after discovering empty kerosene cans in Goodall's camp. Screaming and bristling, Mike charged the other males, banging and rolling the hollow metal cans in front of him. The cans made a terrifying sound that no other chimp could match. Mike became alpha.

At that time, Figan was still young. His older brother, Faben, lost the use of an arm during a polio epidemic that swept through the group in 1966. The disease spread from a nearby African village. As Goodall watched in panic, the disease killed six chimps. One chimp, a bald old male she named Mr. McGregor, pulled himself painfully through the underbrush, his legs dragging uselessly behind him. When he finally dislocated his arm and could no longer get food, Goodall and van Lawick shot him.

Goodall decided to import polio medicine and put it in the bananas she fed the chimps. It was an act that other ethnologists greatly criticized as interference, but it undoubtedly saved some lives.

Now with only one arm, Faben could no longer dominate his younger brother. So the two formed an alliance, with Figan the ruler. In a series of major conflicts, Figan established his dominance as alpha male. Together with Faben, Figan banished his childhood playmate, Evered, by repeatedly ganging up on him.

Next, as Goodall later wrote, Figan took on

Humphrey, a male 15 pounds (7 kilograms) heavier than Figan and a much greater rival. In the gathering twilight, when most of the other chimps were building their nests for the night, Figan made his move. Sucking in his breath and bristling his hair so that he looked larger and more powerful, Figan leaped through the trees, screaming, shaking, and slapping an older male. He then lunged at Humphrey, who was preparing for bed. The two fell 30 feet (9 m) to the ground and Humphrey fled. Figan then attacked two other males. When Humphrey returned and all seemed quiet, Figan attacked him again and once more forced him to flee, screaming.

The community watched the entire demonstration, and Figan had proved that he was the leader. As alpha male, Figan had the choice of females and food. He also settled arguments among other males in the group and maintained social peace. But when Faben disappeared for three weeks—probably on a consortship with a female—Figan was suddenly left alone.

As if fearful of losing his power, Figan acted out often, breaking the morning with his cries. Then he stopped and waited for all members of the group to make a gesture of submission.

For two years, Figan maintained his power, but then Faben disappeared forever. Other males, forming their own alliances, began to demonstrate against Figan, until he too was driven from his position and the cycle started over again.

More mothering. Goodall took some time off so she could raise Grub, her own son.

TIME OF TURMOIL

8

By the early 1970s, the momentous changes occurring in the lives of the chimpanzees matched the changes in Jane Goodall's life. Goodall cut short her research time to raise her son, Grub. There had been accounts of chimpanzees attacking human infants, so Goodall kept Grub away from the chimps. But she was determined to raise her child as she had observed Flo raising hers—with patience and almost constant contact.

At that time, many parents believed that children should be left alone when they cried. But Goodall had watched Flo raise Flint. When Flint grew impatient or threw a tantrum, Flo reassured him, pulled him close and tried to distract him rather than reprimand him. Grub, she decided, would get the same treatment.

During this period, Goodall's marriage to van Lawick was unraveling. The couple spent less time with each other, as Goodall taught at Stanford University and van Lawick worked in West Africa.

"There were basic areas of incompatibility as well," wrote Goodall in *Reason for Hope*. "Of course, we had known about these differences in outlook before we married—but as is the case with most young people, we each believed that our chosen partner would change." When neither partner changed, the gulf between them grew wider, and in 1974, they divorced. Goodall felt tremendous guilt and sorrow when the marriage ended, especially for her son.

Within a year, Goodall married Derek Bryceson, a former Royal Air Force fighter pilot who damaged his spine in a crash during World War II. Rejecting the prognosis that he would remain in a wheelchair, he managed to teach himself to walk with a cane. After the war, Bryceson moved to Tanzania to farm. He earned the loyalty of many people there and was the only white person elected to Tanzania's parliament.

Bryceson was also director of Tanzania's national parks. In 1975, he provided critical help in a crisis that threatened to shut down the Gombe research center.

Kidnapping and Betrayal

Two research assistants had joined Goodall in 1964. But even with their help, it was too much work to observe the chimps and their complex society. In the next ten years, the research center grew. Students from universities in the United States and Europe came to Gombe, usually for six months at a time. They lived in aluminum huts scattered around the camp. At night, the students came together to eat and discuss what they had seen that day.

One night in May 1975, the low growl of a motorboat sounded on Lake Tanganyika. As the sound grew louder, a boat pulled up onto the beach at Gombe. Forty guerrillas, carrying pistols, rifles, and machine guns spilled out of the craft and scrambled into the camp. In the darkness, they spotted the light of a kerosene lamp in one of the huts. They burst into the hut and seized a student who was working late. Then, they entered another hut and startled another student, who cried for help. Two female students responded and were captured. The guerrillas bound their captives and hauled them back to the beach. They loaded their boat, stole the center's only motorboat, and disappeared across the lake.

The kidnappers were guerrillas from Zaire—the new nation across the lake from Tanzania. They had little interest in the center or in what the students were doing there. They reasoned that four white captives would help them in their struggles against the Tanzanian government. A week after the kidnapping, the guerrillas released one student to deliver a message. They demanded $460,000 in cash, a shipment of rifles, and the release of their comrades from prison. If their conditions were not met, they threatened to kill the three remaining students.

A frantic period of negotiations ensued involving the guerrillas, the Tanzanian government, the parents of the students, and Stanford University. After several weeks, the two female students were released for a ransom payment. By the end of August, the fourth student was freed as well, and the nightmare seemed over.

But the center never truly recovered. The crisis had forced the entire research staff to abandon Gombe, taking their research data with them. For several years, Goodall visited the research center only when armed guards accompanied her. The white students were not allowed to return. At any moment, forces outside their control could use them in struggles being waged across Africa. Goodall would not allow this to happen. From then on, Tanzanians recorded field research.

But the fallout over the hostage crisis did not end. When Goodall returned to Stanford University in October 1975, the campus buzzed with nasty rumors that Bryceson had been willing to let the students die. Goodall was shocked, horrified, and hurt, and she tracked down the sources of the rumor to confront them.

When the ordeal ended, Goodall had put most of the rumors to rest, but her teaching at Stanford ended. She also felt the bitterness of betrayal. She wrote in *Reason for Hope*, when she had needed them most, many friends had turned their backs on her. Goodall despaired for human nature. Worse, during that troubled time even her beloved chimps showed behavior that would shock Goodall to the core.

Cannibalism and Warfare

In the early 1970s, researchers observed disturbing attacks by male chimpanzees on solitary females they had found wandering into their territory. In one incident, as Goodall described in *Reason for Hope,* a group of males discovered a foreign female on their southern boundary. She climbed a tree in terror, her infant holding on to her belly. The males surrounded her, and she tried to act submissive. But the gang of males then attacked the female, beat her severely, and killed the infant.

Goodall knew chimps could be violent, but this behavior seemed cruel and unnecessary. All along she had cherished the idea that somehow the chimps were better than humans, more peaceful, more content.

Then, in 1975, Goodall heard a report that shattered her conceptions of chimpanzees. A female chimp named Passion and her daughter, Pom, had been observed stealing an infant away from another chimp in their own group and eating it.

From 1974 to 1978, ten infants were born into the group. Pom and Passion were observed killing five of them. Three others disappeared, and Goodall feared that they too were victims of Pom and Passion. Only when Pom and Passion both gave birth did the cannibalism stop, and Goodall still can't explain why the chimps engaged in such grisly behavior.

But a greater, more violent, conflict had arisen in Gombe. In the early 1970s, a group of chimps—seven adult males and three females—began to spend more and more time in the southern part of the range, eventually forming a separate community. The northern group was called the Kasakela, and the southern group was the Kahama.

Despite their common origins in a single group, the males began to challenge one another when they met in the forest. Usually, the larger group forced the smaller one back to the heart of its territory. "This was typical territorial behavior," wrote Goodall in *Reason for Hope*. "But by 1974, the aggression became more serious."

Six Kasakela chimpanzees slipped silently through the forest toward the southern border. When a young Kahama male, eating alone in a tree, spotted them, he tried to flee. The Kasakela males attacked, holding him to the ground as they stomped and bit him. After ten minutes, they fled, leaving the male seriously wounded. Observers doubt that he recovered. They never saw him again.

For the next four years, the terrifying attacks continued. The Kasakela males eventually tracked down and killed every Kahama male and female. Three childless females were recruited back to Kasakela. Goodall realized that this was not just territorial behavior; this was war—a war of extermination.

Goodall remembered these years as the darkest in Gombe's history. "Our peaceful and idyllic world, our little paradise, had been turned upside down," she wrote in *Reason for Hope*. "They, like us, had a dark side to their nature."

When Goodall reported her observations, many scientists urged her to stay silent. The scientific community—like the chimpanzees of Gombe—had split into warring camps. One group stated that men and women are "blank slates" at birth. Violence and our capacity to love and to hate is learned. If we raised our children without aggression and competition, they argued, we could create a peaceful utopia.

The other scientists insisted that this was nonsense. Human beings, no matter how they're raised, will be in turn loving and violent. It's how we're made.

Anger and aggression. Goodall observed negative behavior that sometimes reminded her of human traits.

Goodall's evidence of "war" in Gombe supported the idea that violence is a part of human nature. Some scientists feared that this would excuse warfare in the world. For Goodall, it was a distressing encounter with the way that politics, religion, and social theories interfered with science.

Death

But after a decade of terror, pain, and disappointment, Goodall faced her greatest test—watching her beloved husband succumb to cancer in 1980. "It was the hardest time, the cruelest time, of my life—watching someone I loved dying slowly, and in pain, from cancer," wrote Goodall in *Reason for Hope*. "I had always believed that this was something I simply could not cope with, but when the time came, I had no choice. I had to watch him get weaker, and suffer, and die."

During this time, as she observed her husband's agony helplessly, Goodall's faith wavered. Goodall had always believed deeply in a compassionate creator—a loving God—no matter which religion God appeared in. But her grief, guilt, and anger overwhelmed her.

She returned to Gombe after Bryceson's death. In the forest silence, broken only by the sounds of animals and the rain and thunder of a passing storm, Goodall found the peace she had been seeking. Her time with the chimps was not spent in observation, but in taking comfort from old friends.

The work at Gombe went on. A student had died in Gombe in 1968, when she wandered over the

Quiet time. After Bryceson's death, Goodall found peace within the African forest.

edge of a cliff. From then on, a guide accompanied all students, in case someone was injured. Many of these guides had become keen observers on their own and knew the ways of the forest. Through their eyes, the research at Gombe continued.

New challenges. As she grew older, Goodall turned her efforts to saving chimpanzees and preserving nature.

VOICE FOR CONSERVATION

I n October 1986, Goodall's life changed forever. After years of having an uneasy relationship with the scientific establishment, Goodall published *The Chimpanzees of Gombe*. Unlike her earlier books, which were aimed at the general reader, *The Chimpanzees of Gombe* was a book filled with charts, graphs, and scientific methods aimed at supporting her broad conclusions about the nature of chimpanzee behavior.

The book was a great success and a conference was held to celebrate the publication. Dozens of biologists working in Africa and some working with captive chimpanzees in the United States attended the conference. For four days, they met and exchanged information about their work with chimpanzees. For Goodall, the conference was life-changing: "When I arrived in Chicago, I was a research scientist. . . . When I left, I was already, in my heart, committed to conservation and education."

Goodall was shocked to learn that chimpanzees were vanishing at an alarming rate. In 1900, as many as 2 million chimps lived in twenty-five nations in Africa. But by 1986, less than 150,000 survived, and they continued to be threatened.

Trees were felled for new buildings, fields were cleared, and roads were built. The human population infected the chimps with their diseases, often with devastating results. A thriving market in chimpanzee meat had developed, and poachers shot chimpanzees by the hundreds. Others killed mother chimps and sold their babies for zoos, circuses, and pets.

These developments had alarmed chimp researchers in Africa, who saw the devastation before their eyes. Many of them were angry that Goodall didn't use her influence to bring world attention to the crisis. Goodall agonized over her chimps in Gombe, but she didn't seem to realize that chimps were being exterminated across Africa.

In 1977, Goodall had founded the Jane Goodall Institute for Wildlife, Research and Conservation. But the center had actually done little conservation work. Goodall, world famous, had never contacted a member of Congress to lobby on behalf of the chimps.

From Observer to Activist

The 1986 conference changed everything. Goodall established the Committee for the Conservation and Care of Chimpazees (CCCC), a group that collected hard evidence that chimps were in danger. For the next two years, she and the CCCC lobbied Congress in Washington, D.C., to declare that chimps were an endangered species, a designation that would offer them more protection around the world.

Goodall also turned her attention to chimpanzees being held in captivity. In the United States, she toured a facility where chimpanzees were kept for medical research. In shock and horror, Goodall peered through tiny slots into cages where infant chimps sat hunched over in depression, despair, and crushing boredom. Though clean and fed, the chimps had little contact with others, no exercise time, and no chance to play. "I am still haunted by the memory of the eyes of [the chimps] I saw that day," wrote Goodall in *Reason for Hope* "They were dull and blank, like the eyes of people who have lost all hope."

Goodall took the cause of the chimpanzee everywhere. She appeared on television shows—*Donahue, Nightline, Good Morning America*—to publicize the plight of the chimp, both in captivity and in the wild. On a tour in the United States in 1987, Goodall visited fourteen cities and six zoos, gave twelve lectures, seven press conferences, seven television interviews, two seminars, and five dinner talks in fifty-two days.

She developed a set of minimum requirements for lab chimpanzees, but the National Institute of Health (NIH) and the U.S. Department of Agriculture refused to implement them. Goodall's defense of animals drew criticism from many who argued that animal experimentation was necessary to save human lives.

At a party, a woman who belonged to a group called People for Animal Experimentation suddenly accosted Goodall. The woman "proceeded to tear strips off me," remembered Goodall in a scene she described in *Reason for Hope*. Her daughter, said the woman, had heart problems and was alive because of medical experiments performed on dogs. If Goodall had her way, the woman claimed, her daughter would be dead. "People like you make me sick," she said.

Goodall replied that her mother, Vanne, was alive only because of a pig valve in her heart. The procedure had been developed on pigs in a laboratory. "I happen to love pigs," said Goodall. "They are quite as intelligent as dogs—often more so. I just feel terribly grateful to the pig who saved my mother's life, and to the pigs who may have suffered to make the operation possible. So I want to do all I can to improve conditions for pigs—in the labs and on the farms. Don't you feel grateful to the dogs who saved your daughter? Wouldn't you like to support efforts to find alternatives so that no more dogs—or pigs—need be used in the future?"

Silence. "No one ever put it like that before," said the woman, her angry expression gone. "I will pass on your message to my group."

As an activist, Goodall maintained a busy schedule, lecturing for months at a time in the United

States. She did not bombard her crowds with statistics and data to prove the danger chimpanzees were facing. Instead, she told stories of chimpanzees, describing their love, their passion, and how they mourn the deaths of relatives. And she did not make generalizations or assign blame for the problem. In her soft, deliberate way of speaking, she considered the dilemma from all sides, gaining the respect of those who disagreed with her and winning many converts.

She understood that medical experiments were meant to ease human suffering. Her beloved husband had died of cancer, and she realized that experiments could one day find a cure for the dreaded disease. But, she argued, there is no point in creating misery among animals to dispel misery among humans.

She also used arguments that were nearly impossible to ignore. A former head of the (NIH) complained that Goodall's proposals, such as expanding cage size and providing comfortable bedding, were too costly. Goodall, in *Reason for Hope*, pointed out that the director worked in a nice office, owned a large house, a car, and took several days of vacation per year. Surely the center, she said, could invest in making the chimps just a little more comfortable too.

Environmentalist

In the 1990s, Goodall turned her attention from saving the chimpanzees to a much larger task—saving ourselves. As she traveled to Gombe year after year, she noticed that more and more of the nearby forest was gone. The trees had been cut down for firewood or for buildings or cleared for crops. The tree roots once anchored the soil, and now the soil washed into the lakes and spoiled the fishing grounds.

These things were happening all over the world.

Learning from nature. After years of study in the wild, Goodall saw that the environment was being destroyed.

Exploding population growth and wasteful economic practices were ruining the landscape and leaving waterways polluted.

Goodall developed a program—Roots and Shoots—to educate the younger generation. Goodall picked the name because roots spread through the ground and form a foundation. Shoots are small and tender plants, but they can break through brick walls. And Goodall described the daunting problems facing our world—poverty, hunger, pollution, greed, crime—as bricks that must be destroyed.

People often wonder how Goodall still has so much energy. Most of her time is spent on the road, lecturing groups, bringing her cause to the greatest number of people. Goodall explains that she gets inspiration from the people she meets. So many of them have overcome obstacles, injuries, or deformities to embrace life. Their energy and their courage inspire her.

Goodall's Legacy

On July 14, 2000, Jane Goodall celebrated the fortieth anniversary of observing chimps in Gombe. Hers is the longest animal-observation study in history. The world has changed in the past forty years, and Goodall is one of the individuals behind that change. She has altered the way we look at ourselves, animals, and our place in the world. And her skill as a communicator has made her name and her discoveries household words. She also changed science by using empathy and compassion, an earthquake to the scientific establishment.

Despite the steady increase of the human population and pollution in the world, Goodall remains optimistic. She has three reasons, she says, for maintaining her hope—our ability to reason; the energy and commitment of young people; and the human spirit. On the Jane Goodall Institute's website, Goodall challenges us with the following words:

So let us move into the next millennium with hope, for without it all we can do is eat and drink the last of our resources as we watch out planet slowly die. Instead, let us have faith in ourselves, in our intellect, in our staunch spirit. Let us develop respect for all living things. Let us try to replace impatience and intolerance with understanding and compassion. And love.

TIMELINE

1934 Jane Goodall born on April 3 in London

1939 Moves with her family to France but soon returns to England

1945 Her parents divorce

1952 Graduates from a private school; spends time in Germany; studies to be a secretary

1956 Receives invitation to visit Africa

1957 Travels to Africa for the first time; meets Louis Leakey

1958 Travels with her mother to Gombe; remains there for the next three years

1961 Is joined in Gombe by her sister, Judy, who is sent to photograph the chimpanzees; returns to England with her research; begins work on her Ph.D.

1962	Returns to Gombe; is joined by *National Geographic* photographer Hugo van Lawick
1963	Receives the National Geographic Society's Franklin Burr Award; receives it the next year as well
1964	Marries van Lawick in March
1967	Gives birth to a son, Hugo Eric Louis, nicknamed Grub
1971	Publishes *In the Shadow of Man*
1974	Divorces van Lawick
1975	Marries Derek Bryceson; students kidnapped in Gombe
1977	Founds the Jane Goodall Institute for Wildlife Research and Conservation
1980	Bryceson dies from cancer
1986	Publishes *Chimpanzees of Gombe*; makes a commitment to conservation
1987	Tours the United States talking about chimpanzees
1999	Publishes *Reason for Hope*

HOW TO BECOME AN ANTHROPOLOGIST

The Job

Anthropology is concerned with the study and comparison of people in all parts of the world, their physical characteristics, customs, languages, traditions, material possessions, and social and religious beliefs and practices. Anthropologists constitute the smallest group of social scientists, yet they cover the widest range of subject matter.

Anthropological data may be applied to solving problems in human relations in fields such as industrial relations, race and ethnic relations, social work, political administration, education, public health, and programs involving transcultural or foreign relations. Anthropology can be broken down into subsets: cultural anthropology, linguistic anthropology, and physical or biological anthropology.

Cultural anthropology, the area in which the greatest number of anthropologists specialize, deals with human behavior and studies aspects of both extinct and current societies, including religion, language, politics, social structure and traditions, mythology, art, and intellectual life. *Cultural anthropologists,* also called *ethnologists* or *social anthropologists,* classify and compare cultures according to general laws of historical, cultural, and social development. To do this effectively, they often work with smaller, perhaps less diverse societies. For example, a cultural anthropologist might decide to study Romany of eastern Europe, interviewing and observing Romany in Warsaw, Prague, and Bucharest. Or, a cultural anthropologist could choose to study Appalachian families of Tennessee and, in addition to library research, would talk to people in Appalachia to learn about family structure, traditions, morals, and values.

Physical anthropologists, also called biological anthropologists, are concerned primarily with the biology of human groups. They study the differences between the members of past and present human societies and are particularly interested in the geographical distribution of human physical characteristics. They apply their intensive training in human anatomy to the study of human evolution and establish differences between races and groups of people. Physical anthropologists can apply their training to forensics or genetics, among other fields. Their work on the effect of heredity and environment on cultural attitudes toward health and nutrition enables medical anthropologists to help develop urban health programs.

One of the most significant contributions of physical anthropologists comes from their research on nonhuman primates. Knowledge about the social organization, dietary habits, and reproductive behaviors of chimpanzees, gorillas, baboons, and others helps explain a great deal about human behavior, motivation, and origins. People working in primate studies are increasingly interested in conservation issues because the places where primates live are threatened by development and the overharvesting of forest products. The work done by Jane Goodall is a good example of this type of anthropology.

Requirements

High School Follow your high school's college prep program to be prepared for undergraduate and graduate programs in anthropology. You should study English composition and literature to develop your writing and interpretation skills. Foreign language skills will also help you in later research and language study. Take classes in computers, and classes in sketching, simple surveying, and photography to prepare for some of the demands of fieldwork. Mathematics and science courses can help you develop the skills you'll need in analyzing information and statistics.

Postsecondary Training You should be prepared for a long training period beyond high school. More anthropologists are finding jobs with only master's degrees, but most of the better positions in anthropology will require a doctorate, which entails about four to six years of work beyond the bachelor's degree. You'll need a doctorate in order to join the faculty of college and university anthropology programs. Before beginning graduate work, you will study such basic courses as psychology, sociology, history, geography, mathematics, logic, English composition, and literature, as well as modern and ancient languages. The final two years of the undergraduate program will provide an opportunity for specialization not only in anthropology but in some specific phase of the discipline.

Students planning to become physical anthropologists should concentrate on the biological sciences. A wide range of interdisciplinary study in languages, history, and the social sciences, as well as the humanities, is particularly important in cultural anthropology, including the areas of linguistics and ethnology. Independent field study also is done in these areas.

In starting graduate training, you should select an institution that has a good program in the area in which you hope to specialize. This is important, not only because the training should be of a high quality, but because most graduates in anthropology will receive their first jobs through their graduate universities.

Assistantships and temporary positions may be available to holders of bachelor's or master's degrees but are usually available only to those working toward a doctorate.

Other Requirements

You should be able to work as part of a team, as well as conduct research entirely on your own. Because much of your career will involve study and research, you should have great curiosity and a desire for knowledge.

Exploring

Anthropology may be explored in a number of ways. For example, Boy Scout and Girl Scout troops participate in camping expeditions for exploration purposes. Local amateur anthropological societies may have weekly or monthly meetings and guest speakers, study developments in the field, and engage in exploration on the local level. You may begin to learn about other cultures on your own by attending local cultural festivals, music and dance performances, and cultural celebrations and religious ceremonies that are open to the public.

Trips to museums also will introduce you to the world of anthropology. Both high school and college students may work in museums on a part-time basis during the school year or during summer vacations. The Earthwatch Institute offers some great opportunities for student anthropologists—its Student Challenge Awards program gives selected students opportunities to assist in the summer research of scientists. Recent projects have included an archeological study with computer imaging at an ancestral Hopi village and a study of rock art of the Malheur Marshlands in eastern Oregon.

Employers

Traditionally, most anthropologists have worked as professors for colleges, universities, and community colleges, or as curators for museums. But these numbers are changing. The American Anthropological Association (AAA) estimates that while about 70 percent of their professional members still work in academia, about 30 percent work in such diverse areas as social service programs, health organizations, city planning departments, and marketing departments of corporations. Some also work as consultants.

Starting Out

The most promising way to gain entry into these occupations is through graduate school. Graduates in anthropology might be approached prior to graduation by prospective employers. Often, professors will provide you with introductions as well as recommendations. You may have an opportunity to work as a research assistant or a teaching fellow while in graduate school, and frequently this experience is of tremendous help in qualifying for a job in another institution. The AAA newsletter includes job listings; it also posts job listings at its annual meetings.

You should also be involved in internships to gain experience; these internship opportunities may be available through your graduate program, or you may have to seek them out yourself. Many organizations can benefit from the help of an anthropology student—health centers, government agencies, and environmental groups all conduct research.

Advancement

Because of the relatively small size of this field, advancement is not likely to be fast, and the opportunities for advancement may be somewhat limited. Most people beginning their teaching careers in colleges or universities will start as instructors and eventually advance to assistant professor, associate professor, and possibly full professor. Researchers on the college level have an opportunity to head research areas and to gain recognition among colleagues as an expert in many areas of study.

Anthropologists employed in museums also have an opportunity to advance within the institution in terms of raises in salary or increases in responsibility and job prominence. Those anthropologists working outside academia and museums will be promoted according to the standards of the individual companies and organizations for which they work.

Earnings

According to the U.S. Department of Labor, college and university professors generally earned between $33,390 and $71,360, depending on the type of institution. A 1998–99 survey by the American Asssociation of University Professors reported that the average salary for full-time professors was about $56,300. For those working outside of academia, the salaries vary widely. The National Association for the Practice of Anthropology (a segment of the AAA) estimates that anthropologists with bachelor's degrees will start at about $16,000 a year; with five years experience they can make $20,000 a year. Those with doctorates will start at about $25,000, working up to $30,000 with five years' experience. Midcareer anthropologists have annual salaries of between $35,000 and $75,000. Salaries in urban areas are somewhat higher. As faculty members, anthropologists and archaeologists benefit from standard academic vacation, sick leave, and retirement plans.

Work Environment

The majority of anthropologists are employed by colleges and universities and, as such, have good working conditions, although fieldwork may require extensive travel and difficult living conditions. Educational facilities are normally clean, well lighted, and ventilated.

Anthropologists work about forty hours a week, and the hours may be irregular. Physical strength and stamina is necessary for fieldwork of all types. Those working on excavations, may work during most of the daylight hours and spend the evening planning the next day's activities. Those engaged in teaching may spend many hours in laboratory research or in preparing lessons to be taught. The work is interesting, however, and those employed in the field are usually highly motivated and unconcerned about long, irregular hours or primitive living conditions.

Outlook

Most new jobs arising in the near future will be non-teaching positions in consulting firms, research institutes, corporations, and federal, state, and local government agencies. Among the factors contributing to this growth is increased environmental, historic, and cultural preservation legislation. There is a particular demand for people with the ability to write environmental impact statements. You'll have to be creative in finding work outside of academia and convincing employers that your training in anthropology makes you uniquely qualified for the work. For these jobs, you'll be competing with people from a variety of disciplines. Positions available in nonacademic areas as well as a limited number of teaching jobs make the expected growth rate for this field to be about as fast as average through 2008, according to the U.S. Department of Labor.

TO LEARN MORE ABOUT ANTHROPOLOGISTS

Books

Gardner, Robert. *Human Evolution.* Danbury, Conn.: Franklin Watts, 1999.

Poynter, Margaret. *The Leakeys: Uncovering the Origins of Humankind.* Springfield, N.J.; Enslow, 1997.

Ziesk, Edra. *Margaret Mead: Anthropologist.* New York: Chelsea House, 1990.

Websites

American Anthropological Association (AAA)
http://www.ameranthassn.org
For a great deal of valuable information about the career and current issues affecting anthropologists; AAA also has a student association.

Earthwatch Institute
http://www.earthwatch.org
The website of the nonprofit organization dedicated to the environment and saving it

Society for Applied Anthropology (SFAA)
http://www.sfaa.net
A respected internation organization in the field of anthropology

Where to Write
American Anthropological Association (AAA)
4350 North Fairfax Drive, Suite 640
Arlington, VA 22203
703-528-1902
To find out more about an anthropology career

Earthwatch Institute
3 Clock Tower Place, Suite 100
P.O. Box 75
Maynard, MA 01754
Email: info@earthwatch.org
To learn more about the Student Challenge Awards and the other programs available

Society for Applied Anthropology (SFAA)
P.O. Box 24083
Oklahoma City, OK 73124
Email: info@sfaa.net
To learn more about this diversified group

HOW TO BECOME A WRITER

The Job

Writers are involved with the expression, editing, promoting, and interpreting of ideas and facts. Their work appears in books, magazines, trade journals, newspapers, technical studies and reports, company newsletters, radio and television broadcasts, and even advertisements.

Writers develop ideas for plays, novels, poems, and other related works. They report, analyze, and interpret facts, events, and personalities. They also review art, music, drama, and other artistic presentations. Some writers persuade the general public to choose certain goods, services, and personalities.

Writers work in the field of communications. Specifically, they deal with the written word for the printed page, broadcast, computer screen, or live theater. Their work is as varied as the materials they produce: books, magazines, trade journals, newspapers, technical reports, company newsletters and other publications, advertisements, speeches, scripts for motion-picture and stage productions, and for radio and television broadcasts.

Prose writers for newspapers, magazines, and books do many similar tasks. Sometimes they come up with their own idea for an article or book and sometimes they are assigned a topic by an editor. Then they gather as much information as possible about the subject through library research, interviews, the Internet, observation, and other methods. They make notes from which they gather material for their project. Once the material has been organized, they prepare a written outline. The process of developing a piece of writing involves detailed and solitary work, but it is exciting.

When they are working on an assignment, writers submit their outlines to an editor or other company representative for approval. Then they write a first draft of the manuscript, trying to put the material into words that will have the desired effect on their readers. They often rewrite or polish sections of the material, always searching for just the right way of getting the information across or expressing an idea or opinion. A manuscript may be reviewed, corrected, and revised numerous times before a final copy is submitted.

Writers for newspapers, magazines, or books often specialize in a specific subject. Some writers might have an educational background that allows them to give a critical interpretation or analysis. For example, a health or science writer typically has a degree in biology and can interpret new ideas in the field for the average reader.

Screenwriters prepare scripts for motion pictures or television. They select—or are assigned—a subject, conduct research, write and submit a plot outline or story, and discuss possible revisions with the producer and/or director. Screenwriters may adapt books or plays for film and television. They often collaborate with other screenwriters and may specialize in a particular type of script. Playwrights write for the stage. They create dialogue and describe action for comedies and dramas. Themes are sometimes adapted from fictional, historical, or narrative sources. Playwrights combine action, conflict, purpose, and resolution to tell stories of real or imaginary life. They often make revisions even while the play is in rehearsal.

Continuity writers prepare material for radio and television announcers to introduce or connect various parts of their programs.

Novelists and short-story writers create stories for books, magazines, or literary journals. They use incidents from their own lives, from news events, or from their imagination to create characters, settings, and actions. Poets create narrative, dramatic, or lyric poetry for books, magazines, or other publications, as well as for special events such as commemorations.

Requirements

High School   High-school courses that are helpful for a writer include English, literature, foreign languages, general science, social studies, computer science, and typing. The ability to type and familiarity with computers are almost requisites for positions in communications.

Postsecondary   Competition for work as a writer almost always demands the background of a college education.

Many employers prefer people who have a broad liberal arts background or a major in English, literature, history, philosophy, or one of the social sciences. Some employers prefer communications or journalism training in college. Occasionally a master's degree in a specialized writing field may be required. A number of colleges and schools offer courses in journalism, and some of them offer courses in book publishing, publication management, and newspaper and magazine writing.

In addition to formal education, most employers look for practical writing experience. If you have worked on high-school or college newspapers, yearbooks, or literary magazines, you will make a better candidate. Work for small community newspapers or radio stations, even in an unpaid position, is also an advantage. Many book publishers, magazines, newspapers, and radio and television stations have summer internship programs. These provide valuable training if you want to learn about the publishing and broadcasting businesses. Interns do many simple tasks, such as running errands and answering phones, but some may be asked to perform research, conduct interviews, or even write some minor pieces.

Writers who specialize in technical fields may need degrees, concentrated course work, or experience in their subject areas. This usually applies to engineering, business, and the sciences. Also, a degree in technical communications is now offered at many colleges.

If you want a position with the federal government, you will be required to take a civil service examination and meet specific requirements, according to the type and level of the position.

Other Requirements   Writers should be creative and able to express ideas clearly, have broad general knowledge, be skilled in research techniques, and be computer-literate. Other assets include curiosity, persistence, initiative, resourcefulness, and an accurate memory. For some jobs—on a newspaper, for example, where the activity is hectic and the deadlines are short—the ability to concentrate and produce under pressure is essential.

Exploring

As a high-school or college student, you can test your interest and aptitude in the field by working as a reporter or writer on school newspapers, yearbooks, and literary magazines. Various writing courses, workshops, and books help you to sharpen your writing skills.

Small community newspapers and local radio stations often welcome contributions from outside sources, although they may not have the resources to pay for them. Jobs in bookstores, magazine shops, and even newsstands can help you become familiar with the various publications.

Information on writing as a career may also be obtained by visiting local newspapers, publishers, or radio and television stations. You may interview some of the writers who work there. Career conferences and other guidance programs often have speakers on the field of communications from local or national organizations.

Employers

Nearly one-third of salaried writers and editors work for newspapers, magazines, and book publishers, according to the *Occupational Outlook Handbook*. Many writers work for advertising agencies, in radio and television broadcasting, or in public relations firms. Others work on journals and newsletters published by business and non-profit organizations. Other employers include government agencies and film-production companies.

Starting Out

Experience is required to gain a high-level position in this field. Most writers start out in entry-level jobs. These jobs may be listed with college placement offices, or you may apply directly to publishers or broadcasting companies. Graduates who have previously served internships with these companies often know someone who can give them a personal recommendation.

Employers in the communications field are usually interested in samples of your published writing. These may be assembled in an organized portfolio or scrapbook. Bylined or signed articles are more helpful than those whose source is not identified.

A beginning position as a junior writer usually involves library research, preparation of rough drafts for a report, cataloging, and other related writing tasks. These are generally carried on under the supervision of a senior writer.

Advancement

Most writers start out as editorial or production assistants. Advancement is often more rapid in small companies, where beginners learn by doing a little of everything and may be given writing tasks immediately. In large firms, however, duties are usually more compartmentalized. Assistants in entry-level positions do research, fact-checking, and copyrighting, but it generally takes much longer to advance to writing tasks.

Promotion into a more responsible position may come with the assignment of more important articles and stories, or it may be the result of moving to another company. Employees in this field often move around. An assistant in one publishing house may switch to an executive position in another. Or a writer may advance by switching to a related field: for example, from publishing to teaching, public relations, advertising, radio, or television.

Freelance or self-employed writers may advance by earning larger fees as they widen their experience and establish their reputation.

Work Environment

Working conditions vary for writers. Although the workweek usually runs thirty-five to forty hours, many writers work overtime. A publication that is issued frequently has more deadlines closer together, which creates greater pressures. The work is especially hectic on newspapers and at broadcasting companies, which operate seven days a week. Writers often work nights and weekends to meet deadlines or to cover a late-developing story.

Most writers work independently, but often they must cooperate with artists, photographers, rewriters, and advertising people. These people may have widely differing ideas of how the materials should be prepared and presented.

The work is sometimes difficult, but writers are seldom bored. Each day brings new and interesting problems. The jobs occasionally require travel. The most difficult aspect is the pressure of deadlines. People who are the most content as writers enjoy and work well under deadline pressure.

Earnings

In 1998, median annual earning for writers were $36,480 a year, according to the *Occupational Outlook Handbook.* Salaries range from $20,920 to $76,660.

In addition to their salaries, many writers earn some income from freelance work. Part-time freelancers may earn from $5,000 to $15,000 a year. Freelance earnings vary widely. Full-time established freelance writers may earn up to $75,000 a year.

Outlook

Employment in this field is expected to increase faster than the average rate of all occupations through 2008. The demand for writers by newspapers, periodicals, book publishers, and nonprofit organizations is expected to increase.

The major book and magazine publishers, broadcasting companies, advertising agencies, public relations firms, and the federal government account for the large number of writers in cities such as New York, Chicago, Los Angeles, Boston, Philadelphia, San Francisco, and Washington, D.C. Opportunities in small newspapers, corporations, and professional, religious, business, technical, and trade publications can be found throughout the United States.

TO LEARN MORE ABOUT WRITERS

Books

Fletcher, Ralph B. *A Writer's Notebook: Unlocking the Writer within You*. New York: Camelot, 1996.

Janeczko, Paul B. *How to Write Poetry*. New York: Scholastic, 1999.

Krull, Kathleen. *Lives of the Writers: Tragedies, Comedies*. Austin: Raintree/Steck-Vaughn, 1998.

New Moon Books Girls Editorial Board. *Writing: How to Express Yourself with Passion and Practice*. New York: Crown, 2000.

Reeves, Diane Lindsey. *Career Ideas for Kids Who Like Writing*. New York: Facts On File, 1998.

Stevens, Carla. *A Book of Your Own: Keeping a Diary or Journal*. New York: Clarion, 1993.

Websites
Creative Writing for Teens
http://teenwriting.about.com
Tips, news, activities, a chat room, and a selection of young authors' works

4Writers
http://www.4writers.com
Support for professional and aspiring writers, plus information about conferences, artists' colonies, and the top creative writing programs

Writer's Digest
http://www.writersdigest.com
Features daily writing and publishing updates, plus information about the best places to get published

Where to Write
National Association of Science Writers
P.O. Box 294
Greenlawn, NY 11740
516/757-5664
For information on writing and editing careers in the field of communications

National Conference of Editorial Writers
6223 Executive Boulevard
Rockville, MD 20852
301/984-3015
For information about student memberships available to those interested in opinion writing

PEN American Center
568 Broadway
New York, NY 10012-3225
Helps foster writers of literary works and provides awards, grants, and support

Tallwood House
MSN 1E3
George Mason University
Fairfax, VA 22030
Provides support for writers and a directory of writing programs

Writers Guild of America
7000 West Third Street
Los Angeles, CA 90048
For information about this organization that represents writers of all kinds

TO LEARN MORE ABOUT JANE GOODALL

Books

Burby, Liza N. *Jane Goodall: Leading Animal Behaviorist.* New York: Rosen, 1997.

Goodall, Jane. *The Chimpanzee Family Book.* New York: North-South Books, 1997.

————. *My Life with Chimpanzees.* New York: Pocket, 1996.

————. *With Love: Ten Heartwarming Stories of Chimpanzees in the Wild.* New York: North-South Books, 1998.

Pettit, Jane. *Jane Goodall: Pioneer Researcher.* Danbury, Conn.: Franklin Watts, 1999.

Websites
ChimpanZoo
http://chimpanzoo.arizona/edu/
For information about this program sponsored by the Jane Goodall Institute

The Jane Goodall Institute
http://www.janegoodall.org/
The official website about Goodall's life and work

Jane Goodall: The Great Conservationist
http://www.wic.org/bio/jgoodall.htm
A biography of Goodall sponsored by the Women's International Center

An Interesting Place to Visit
Busch Gardens
3605 Bougainvillea Avenue
Tampa, Florida 33612
813/987-5082
To see some of Africa's primates up close

INDEX

Page numbers in *italics* indicate illustrations.

ABOUT THE AUTHOR

Brendan January graduated from Haverford College and Columbia University Graduate School of Journalism. He has written several nonfiction books for young readers, including one recognized as a Best Science Book of 1999 by the National Science Teachers Association. Brendan January is currently a journalist at the *Philadelphia Inquirer* and lives with his wife in New Jersey.